TO SAVANNAH, TJ AND ALIZA: You were fearfully and wonderfully created by our Heavenly Father; don't ever forget that you are amazing just the way you are. Work hard, never give up on your dreams and always do your very best.

THANKS TO: Admiral (retired) Erroll Brown for allowing me the opportunity to feature him in my first children's book and for being a great mentor to many including myself.

~ SEA

_____

_____

Library of Congress Control Number: 2014951080

Erroll Mingo Brown was born in Ocala, Florida in the summer of 1950. Erroll's grandparents raised him in a tiny old house surrounded by trees and dirt roads in a small town near the city.

They did not have much money growing up. His grandfather earned a living as a farmer. His grandmother worked as a cook at a local restaurant.

When Erroll was born, he was diagnosed with double-pneumonia. This was a very scary time for the family because many sick babies died of pneumonia back in those days. They thought he was going to die too.
Every day, the family prayed for Erroll to get well.

One day when he was about three years old, the doctor declared that he was in good health! The family was so happy that God listened to their prayers. They were thankful because God spared his life.

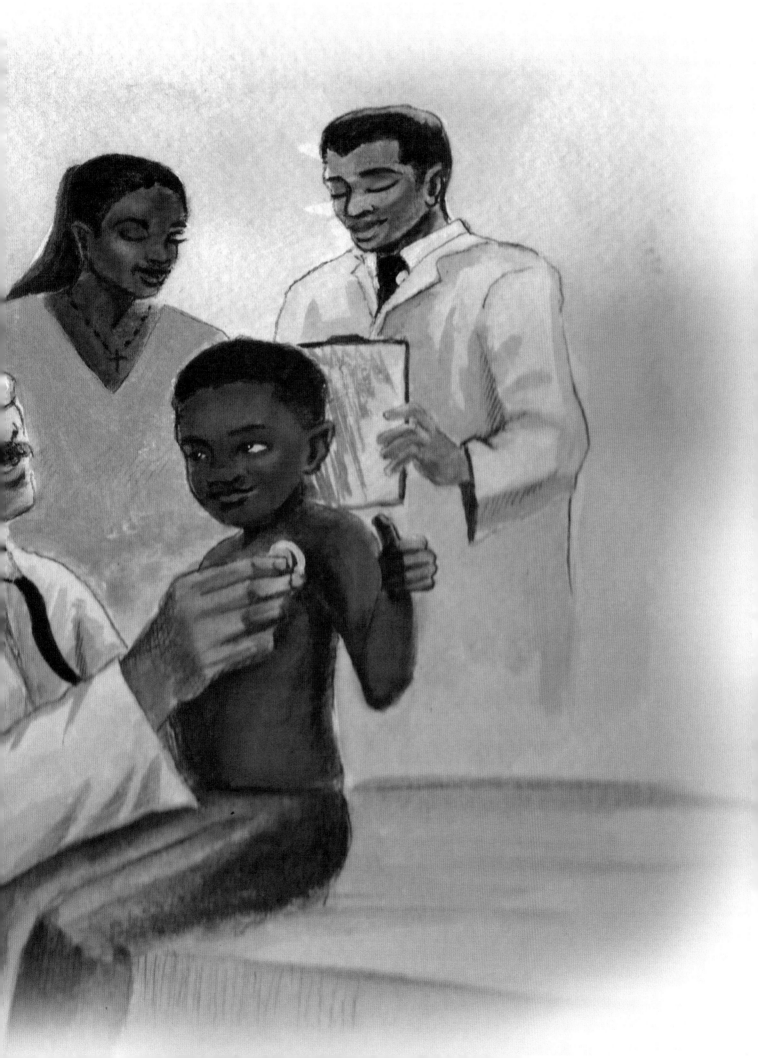

When Erroll was old enough, he was assigned chores around the house. Every day, Erroll had to wash, dry and fold clothes, rake the front lawn, mow the grass and hoe the flower beds. Sometimes Erroll had to work out in the fields or pick oranges in the orange grove with his grandfather.

At first, it was hard to finish all of his chores because Erroll was so small and so much younger than everyone else. But he was determined to do his share of the work and before long he was able to finish all of his chores by himself. When Erroll was done with his chores, he was allowed to go out and play with friends. Erroll never complained about helping his family.

One day Erroll hurt himself while helping his brother and cousins in the orange grove. Erroll did not like being hurt because he could not help his family. Then, he had an idea. He asked his grandfather if he could help drive the tractor.

His grandfather refused and told Erroll that he was too little to reach the pedals and drive the tractor. But Erroll insisted;

You can reach the pedals, Grand daddy. If I sit in your lap, I can reach the steering wheel and still see the field among the trees.

After some thought, his grandfather decided to give it a try. In no time, Erroll had learned how to steer the tractor and helped plow every row in the orange grove. His idea worked! After they finished their work in the orange grove, his grandfather gave Erroll a big hug and thanked him for all the hard work he did. Erroll was so proud that day.

Erroll worked hard, but he played hard too! He loved to play basketball, baseball and football. He loved to play with his brother and cousins. Everyone he played with was always taller than Erroll but that didn't bother Erroll one bit! Erroll did not care that he was the smallest player on the team. He just cared about doing his best.

When Erroll was about six years old, he started school. Erroll always listened to his teachers, completed his school work and stayed out of trouble. Erroll was not afraid to raise his hand and ask questions when he did not understand his lessons. The teachers were very fond of him because he was a bright student. He loved to read and he especially loved math!

But Erroll's love for learning extended beyond the classroom. One day his brother and cousins were building a new play house in the woods. Erroll wanted to help them but his brother and cousins told him he was too little. Erroll did not like being told he could not do something. When his brother and cousins went inside the house for lunch, Erroll stayed out in the woods and tried to build the new play house himself. He wanted to show his brother and cousins he could do anything they could do!

Erroll tried to hammer a nail into a wooden board but he kept missing the board and hitting his fingers. When his brother came into the woods to look for him, he was surprised to see Erroll standing there with his fingers bleeding.

He loved Erroll very much and did not like to see him hurt. He decided to teach Erroll the correct way to use a hammer and a nail. Erroll learned quickly and became so good at it that his brother and cousins allowed him to help build the play house.

When Erroll was 8 years old, his mother came home with great news; after many years of college and working part-time, she successfully completed her bachelor's degree in education! She told Erroll and his brother that it was time to move to another city where she had a new job as a school teacher. Erroll loved his mother dearly, but he was sad to leave his grandparents and his cousins.

His mom eventually moved the boys to St Petersburg, Florida where she remarried. They bought a nice home near an elementary school. Soon everyone in the neighborhood knew the family and Erroll was able to make friends quickly. Erroll was good at making friends because he loved to tell jokes and make people laugh.

But some things were no laughing matter. As Erroll grew older, Erroll learned that he was not allowed to go to certain places because of the color of his skin. Restaurants, movie theatres and public restrooms all held *Colored Only* and *White Only* signs. White children and black children could not attend the same schools.

Because of the country's segregation laws, white people had better schools and jobs than black people. Many people felt this was wrong. Americans marched and protested all over the country. This was a scary time in America because so many people were angry. Some were so angry that they attacked and sometimes killed people that marched and protested against segregation.

But Erroll was too young to become involved in these demonstrations. Instead he spent a lot of time in school. It was very important to him that he did well in school because little Erroll had a big dream; he wanted to go to college and become a great engineer one day.

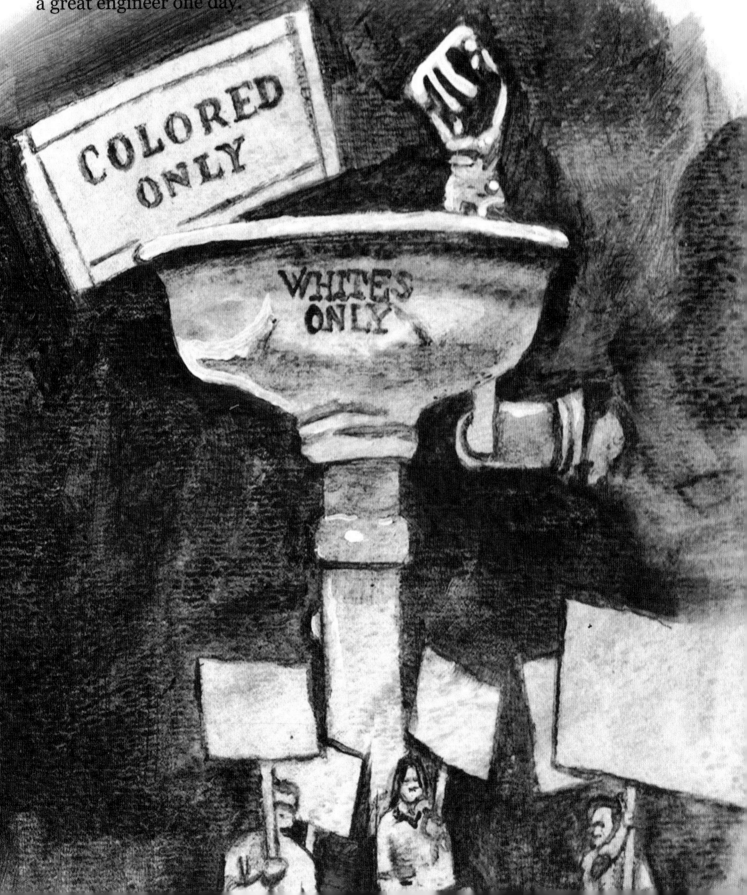

In 1965, Erroll attended a high school in another neighborhood where most of the students were white. Although the laws allowed black and white students to attend the same schools, many people did not accept the new laws. Erroll knew that many of his white classmates did not want him at the high school. Sometimes they teased him.

Erroll ignored the teasing and focused on his dream. Before long, Erroll was placed on the honor roll for having excellent grades. He also played football and was such a great player, that he was placed on the school's hall of fame. Soon, everyone at school liked and respected Erroll.

One day during his senior year in high school, he received a postcard in the mail. It was from a military college called the Coast Guard Academy. He knew it was one of the best colleges in the country so he decided to apply. A few months later he was accepted.

Erroll couldn't wait to go to college! He thought that college would be fun because his mom and dad weren't going to be there to tell him what to do. As he packed his clothes, he imagined his new life; going to parties, eating junk food in his own room, going to bed late and hanging out with his new friends.

But when Erroll stepped through the gates of the Coast Guard Academy in the summer of 1968, he did not see the life he envisioned. Instead he saw scared faces marching and running across campus. He saw his classmates cleaning bedrooms, bathrooms, and sweeping up and down hallways while the older students yelled at them. He saw his classmates sweating and trembling as they tried to do push-ups and sit-ups. Erroll learned quickly that the Coast Guard Academy was different from other colleges.

Erroll had a very tough time his first few months at college. When he received his first report card, it wasn't very good. This was the first time he ever received bad grades in school. Still, when his mother asked him if he wanted to come home, he told her no. Erroll did not want to give up and quit. He knew college was going to be hard but he was determined to do well.

One day he received a visit from a captain in the Coast Guard. This was the first time he ever met a black officer because there were very few black officers in the military in 1970. He was a Coast Guard aviator and he stood very tall and proud in front of him and the other cadets. The captain had so much gold on his uniform that Erroll could not stop blinking his eyes.

The Captain told Erroll that after he finished college, he would be a commissioned officer in the United States Coast Guard. He explained that this was a very important job because the Coast Guard's mission is to protect the country, its citizens and its resources.

As the Captain spoke to the cadets, Erroll thought about all the amazing work that the Coast Guard performs each and every day. He knew his fellow coastguardsmen spent their days and nights at sea, saving lives and keeping the oceans clean. He knew about the dangerous ice patrols that took place in the antarctic and arctic regions in order to keep waterways clear for traveling ships. He even knew about the inspections that took place onboard foreign and domestic seagoing vessels in order to ensure vessel and port safety.

Erroll knew the Coast Guard was a great organization and he looked forward to becoming a commissioned officer after he finished college.

After the visit, Erroll decided that if he worked harder, he could do better in school. By his second year, he excelled academically and received many school awards.

In June 1972, Erroll had successfully completed one of the most rigorous college engineering programs in the entire country. At his graduation ceremony, the Vice President of the United States presented him his officer commission.

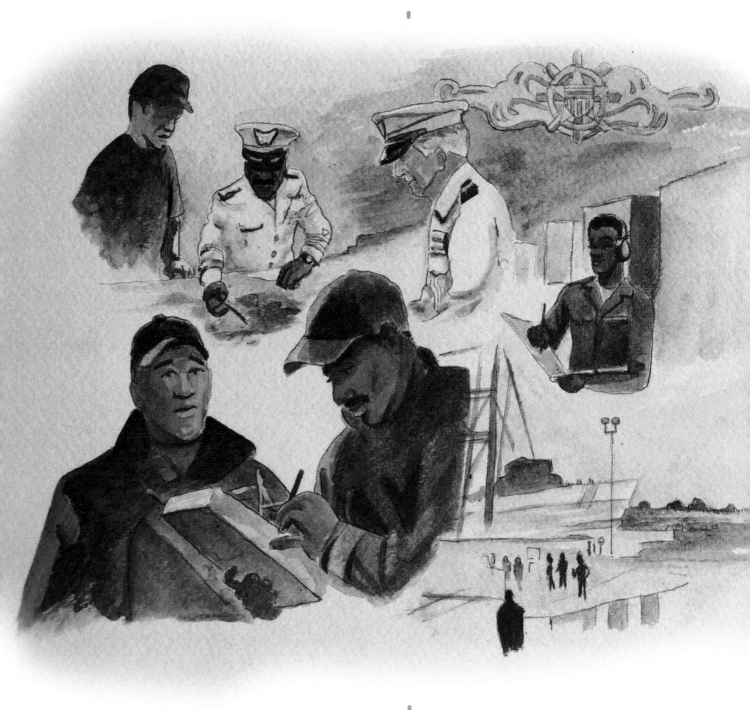

Many years later, Erroll became the first African American in the Coast Guard to ever reach the heights of Admiral; the highest position in the military. He served 33 years in the military before he retired as the Coast Guard's chief engineer. He had a remarkable career. During his retirement ceremony, he celebrated his achievements with family members and friends who loved and respected him greatly:

Our nation stands on the shoulders of engineers...and I am proud to stand here as the #1 engineer in the Coast Guard. Life is a journey of growth and mastery. Master your self-purpose, master your craft and help somebody.

Erroll proved that no matter what your challenges are, you can be whatever it is you want to be.

Glossary of terms

1. Arctic/Antarctic regions: Two very cold areas located near the north and south poles.

2. Aviator: A pilot of an aircraft such as an airplane or helicopter.

3. Coast Guard: The United States Coast Guard (USCG) is a federal uniformed service of the United States Armed Forces.

5. Commissioned Officer: An officer of an armed force with certain leadership authority.

6. Domestic: Nationally-based. From or referring to the United States.

7. Double-Pneumonia (Pneumonia): An infection of the lungs.

8. Engineer: Someone who is trained to design, create or make improvements to an existing device, structure or process.

9. Foreign: Internationally-based. From or referring to a different country.

10. (USCG Marine) Inspection: A safety or security examination of shipboard equipment and personnel aboard a vessel.

11. Mission: A purpose, job or responsibility.

12. Segregation: Racial segregation is the forced separation of people.

13. (Marine) Vessel: A ship or boat.

◇◇◇ Author's Note ◇◇◇

Admiral Erroll M. Brown attended the U.S. Coast Guard Academy from
1968-1972 and majored in Marine Engineering. Upon graduation, he
spent several years at sea aboard; the Coast Guard Icebreaker Burton
Island (WAGB-283) as the Damage Control Assistant & Assistant
Engineer Officer, USCGC Jarvis (WHEC-725) as the Engineer Officer
and the USCGC Rush (WHEC-723) as the Executive Officer. Many years
after serving as a Marine Engineering instructor at the U.S. Coast Guard
Academy, Admiral Brown went on to assume numerous command

positions including; Commanding Officer of the USCG Integrated Support Command,
Portsmouth VA, Commander for the Maintenance Logistics Command Atlantic, Norfolk VA,
District Commander for the Coast Guard 13th District and Assistant Commandant for
Engineering & Logistics. While in the Coast Guard, he earned several degrees including a
Master's degree in Naval Architecture and Marine Engineering and a second Master's degree in
Industrial and Operations Engineering from the University of Michigan, a Master of Business
Administration from the Rensselaer Polytechnic Institute and a Master's degree in National
Security and Strategic Studies from the Naval War College. In 1998, Admiral Brown became the
first African American admiral in Coast Guard history. He retired from the Coast Guard after 33
years of distinguished service in 2005.

Little Erroll is an inspiring biography of Admiral Brown as a child who, despite many challenges,
always found a way to prevail. Whether at school, at home or in the fields helping his Grandpa,
Erroll always did his very best no matter how difficult the situation. This book not only provides
a simple lesson on responsibility and self-purpose but it reminds our young readers that they can
achieve anything with faith, determination and hard work.

About the Author and Illustrator...

Shameen Anthanio-Williams is a graduate of the United States Coast Guard Academy and a Lieutenant Commander in the Coast Guard. She has held a variety of assignments in Marine Safety & Security, Naval Engineering, Acquisitions Management and attended post graduate school at The George Washington University. Born and raised in Bronx, New York, she attended the LaGuardia High School of Music & Art and Performing Arts in Manhattan where her appreciation for creative expression flourished. Shameen, her husband Terence and two children; Savannah and TJ currently reside in Spencerville, Maryland. *Little Erroll* is her first children's book.

Jerome White earned his BA degree in Studio Art at Baldwin-Wallace College, in Berea, Ohio in 1992 and later earned his MA degree, in Art Education, from Case Western Reserve University, in Cleveland, Ohio. He has taught art at Cleveland Heights High School from 1997- 2013 and presently teaches at Roxboro Middle School in Cleveland Heights, Ohio. Jerome is a multi-genre artist who specializes in fine art and murals; his most recent work can be viewed at the Hough Mural at the legendary League Park in Cleveland Ohio. www.jeromesartroom.com

35207312R00020

Made in the USA
Charleston, SC
30 October 2014